I Remember the Robins Chirping

nostalgic memories and letters

By John Winthrop

Printed in the United States of America.

ISBN 978-0-9970242-6-5

J Winthrop, Charleston, South Carolina

www.winthropfamily.org

Dedicated to
Family

PART I

Introduction

Memories of the past fade into the mist too often.
My impulse at the moment is to save a few.

Many of these memories are a bit silly; some are
poignant; a few have helped shape me into a human
being with all the defects or advantages that exist
today. So by its very nature, this literary effort is
rather intimate and precious – to be shared with my
wife, my children, and my grandchildren, as well as
my brother, Matthew.

As we advance in age we tend to reminisce – to look
backwards and to savor the past. In our earlier years
we tend to look forward, to plan for enjoyment, for
family, for various ways to direct our energy.

This is a book of bullet points and letters – bullet
points, or memories, of my own life and letters to my
brother, Matthew, who has had a difficult life.

Both segments belong together because our lives
have been placed together at various intervals
by accident of birth. We are the two oldest of
eight siblings, the two oldest of all Nathaniel T.
Winthrop's offspring.

a few recollections of my

- I remember the robins chirping in the early spring as I went to sleep in our grandparents' safe and secure home in Beverly Farms, Massachusetts.

- My fourth birthday party at my grandparents' home – the frosting on the cake was pink and a toy jack-knife was my most treasured present.

- Walks on Singing Beach in Manchester, Massachusetts, with my brother, Matthew, and our mother.

- The itchy woolen leggings I was forced to wear in Boston by our nurse – a very evil woman. She seemed to enjoy giving us the taste of soap as well.

- Pounding tennis balls into open windows of our second home called Stone Lea in Manchester. Matthew was an expert at this sport.

- The separation and ultimate divorce of our parents.

earliest years . . .

- Our father away in the Navy fighting the German
  and Japanese enemies while I traced the progress
  of the Allied Forces on a map at our home in
  Manchester, Massachusetts. A picture of a B-29
  bomber decorated the wall of my bedroom.

- Mack, our tutor, helping us with carpentry projects.

- "Spats," (a severe slap with a wooden paddle) dished
  out for punishment by Dave Kliever, ex-Marine.

- Fishing off the rocks of our beachfront
  home in Manchester.

- Riding the waves in Singing Beach
  – our greatest joy at the time.

- Getting stung by a bee in the mouth on
  Singing Beach, and, a few days later, falling
  down a rocky cliff outside our home. I cried
  for a long time after each of these events.

from days in Boston, d

- Our difficult adjustment after the divorce of our parents.

- The early days at Dexter School, entering the third grade (with Matthew in first grade).

- Matthew competing with John Nelson for an academic prize in mathematics.

- The love of baseball and the joy of my achievement as a young boy at Dexter (breaking the throwing record for the "Midget" baseball competition).

- The terrifying experience of having to report to the headmaster (after kicking off my shoe and breaking a lamp by mistake while imitating the Nazi goose step).

- Playing football in the gray sweater of the Mohawk team in sports at Dexter school.

- Feeling enormous empathy for Matthew, who tipped over backward and lost much blood from cracking his head on the radiator.

remember . . .

- Going to Harvard with classmate John Finley
  and being brought to Winthrop House by
  his famous father, Professor Finley.

- Wearing red Dexter hats on the bus to school
  from our home on Marlboro Street.

- Matthew's snowball attack on a McKann
  car limousine outside our home in
  Boston (infuriating the driver).

- Drawing pictures of U.S. airplanes attacking
  Japanese zeros with classmate Harry Thayer.

- Getting my first camera as a Christmas
  present from Aunt Theo.

from New York and Buck-

- Our introduction to our new home at 770 Park Avenue, where we were to live with our father and "Miss Dice" - a governess.

- The wonder of seeing cars passing far below our fifth floor apartment on Park Avenue.

- The arrival of wonderful Aunt Nina (Countess Moltke), who was to help shape my early years in this new home.

- The arrival of my dog Tessie, who was to be my full responsibility and who became a devoted pet. (She eventually died while I was in the Navy.)

- Early days at Buckley with friends Curtiss Scarritt, Hayden Conner, Bill Mateleine, Pierre de Vegh, and many more.

- Dodge ball and "battlefield" at Buckley, my favorite sports at the time, along with baseball.

ey School, I remember . . .

- Difficulty with homework in mathematics
  followed by frustrating tutorials with our father
  who was so accomplished at math and physics,
  while I experienced problems with both.

- Trips to Uncle Bob and Aunt Meg's pool in the
  summer time (they rarely appeared on the scene).

- A trip to Bermuda on the *Queen of Bermuda* with
  Mr. Toemey, Harold Block, and Pierre de Vegh
  – with occasional vomits in our stateroom caused
  by seasickness. (This was not a joyful trip!).

- Hurling toys and grapefruits out of Curtiss Scarritt's
  window, causing horror and chaos below.

- Saturday club and Cub Scout meetings
  (to keep young boys out of trouble).

- The marriage of our father to
  Eleanor Beane from Boston.

from Saint Mark's School,

- The feeling of having to make it on my own in a new place, while a new family was being created by my father and Eleanor.

- My inability to compete with the best of Saint Mark's baseball players.

- A solid friendship with Curtiss Scarritt – the only fellow transplant from Buckley, aside from John J. Mortimer.

- The discovery of an unexpected talent within myself in wrestling, followed by three years of undefeated varsity competition. This seemed like a big deal at the time, and made up for my failure in baseball.

- Fixation on grades, grades, grades, so I could get into a decent college.

- The spiritual side of life took on new meaning (along with confirmation in the church).

- Letters from Suzy Ray, my first girlfriend, were treasured for a while along with frequent letters from our mother. (Curtiss and Julia Roosevelt were an item.)

$\mathscr{I}$ remember . . .

- Being elected captain of the wrestling team
  built some self confidence, along with a
  letter in soccer. So much for sports.

- Summer visits to Beverly Farms and a growing
  fondness of for my stepfather, Bartlett Harwood,
  gave me a sense of direction and support I needed.
  This was about the only time Matthew and I could
  play and bond together during our teenage years.

- Acceptance to Harvard was a nice reward at the
  end of my four difficult years at St. Mark's.

- I left the school with an unexpected prize – the Seton
  Porter reward for tenacity and for best fulfilling
  the school motto – *Age Quod Agis* – (Do what
  you do well). What a nice memory that was!

- While my mother loved me and spoiled me,
  she made me give the $100 which came with the
  Seton Porter prize to Saint Mark's as a gift.

and from Harvard . . .

- Freshman year in Wigglesworth with many new friends and some outrageous incidents. It was about this time that Matthew dropped out of Solebury School.

- Mortimer, Davis and Church pointing an ROTC rifle at innocent street walkers, while Wagnerian music played loudly in the background.

- Bob Montgomery's early marriage to Ginger Patterson, followed by a drunken brawl weekend starring John Davis and Dan Morgan.

- Winning the freshman wrestling honors, but losing a few on the Harvard varsity team.

- Election to all the leading clubs, but deciding on Porcellian after weighing Bart's and Lou McCagg's advice. This seemed so important at the time.

- Various jobs taken to support the club bills (at our father's insistence) at Dexter School as a coach; at J. August, a clothier, packing suits; and, finally, selling Cutco cutlery door-to-door. My father held me to a very strict budget. I always tried to please him.

- Struggling with my work – especially
  in the beginning (in our small English
  comp class, Erich Segal was a star).

- Trips to Cuba, to Russia, to Bermuda, and
  to Lana Labelle Farm in Pennsylvania,
  created bonding relationships.

- These were the golden years for Groton Plantation,
  where my father generously allowed me to invite
  many friends, shoot quail and raise hell.

- Two friends, George Ellison and Godfrey Truslow
  (both now deceased), almost got me kicked out of
  Harvard for reasons I wish I was at liberty to disclose.

- Treasuring the solid relationship of
  friends at Harvard, including Heard,
  Clark, Krogh, Davis and others.

- More trips to Groton Plantation in my spare time
  and, finally, acceptance into the U.S. Navy.

from the days in the U.S.

- Dreaming of becoming an officer on our aircraft carrier in the Pacific.

- Reporting for duty and OCS two weeks after graduation.

- Growing difficulties in Newport with the realization that graduates were heading for the Atlantic-based destroyers.

- Accepting the painful decision to flunk and rationalize that I would become a better officer after experiencing the rigors of being an enlisted man.

- Going to boot camp in Great Lakes – lead man on the hose fighting a fire – strep throat in the infirmary.

- Assignment to destroyer tender Sierra AD 18 out of Norfolk (the same ship that carried my father home from WW II).

Navy . . .

- Writing the ship's newspaper and eventually hosting my own radio program. Meanwhile, brother Matthew was writing me many cards and letters.

- Mediterranean Cruise and upgrading to Journalist Third Class.

- Guantanamo Bay cruise after liberty on Virginia Beach on weekends.

- Fear of war over Berlin as we were ordered to go on a transatlantic cruise on the USS Sierra (AD-18).

- The joy of receiving an honorable discharge and acceptance into Columbia MBA program.

- Launching an amateur's career in broadcasting and journalism – both of which provided a creative outlet in the years to come.

business school years and

- Difficulty with Professor Bastable in Accounting & Statistics.

- Satisfaction in Manpower essay with Professor Ginsberg.

- St. Anthony Hall (a fraternity) as a refuge and as an eating club.

- Small apartment uptown on West Side as first perch.

- Kennedy inaugural on TV in 1960 ... a very exciting time.

- Summer job at Citibank in London job with George Parker and Kelly Anderson.

Washington . . .

- Butler as roommate in second year.

- Atlantic Council job with Christian Herter and Cabot Lodge, and move to Washington, DC.

- Occasional breakfast in the White House during the Kennedy years.

- Marriage to Deborah in Sewickley, Pennsylvania.

- Trip around world before settling in New York and writing a series of articles for _The Boston Globe_ – a major event before going to Wall Street!

- Acceptance of a job at Wood, Struthers & Winthrop, necessitating a departure from Washington, DC.

- Began seeing more of brothers, but realizing more and more that Matthew might require special attention.

WSW and divorce . . .

- First day of work in January with Steve Schwartz
  as roommate (and $5,000 annual pay).

- Difficulty in research department
  under Galban and Jones.

- Bob Wood's tutelage in investment advisory
  department, introducing me to more interesting work.

- Attentive to R.W. and R. George,
  fearful of G. Copp and Oakley Brooks,
  friendly with nearly all co-workers.

- Blackout night in 1969 – long
  walk uptown to get home.

- Unable to control my wife's spending
  spree and other problems at home.

- Served with papers for divorce.

- Peter French and Sam LaFace as indispensible
  friends along with Arthur Field.

- Admission as a partner, leading to a leadership role
  in the investment advisory department. (Sherry
  before lunch on Mondays was always a high point!)

- Rapid decline of the other segments of business at WS&W, and eventual merger with DLJ, after consideration of F.S. Mosley, White Weld and other possible merger candidates at the time.

- Meanwhile – through all of this – broadening of my perspective through board work on Green Bay & Western Railroad, NUI Utility, Groton Land Company, and Wood, Struthers & Winthrop … also in the not-for-profit arena, Fresh Air Fund, Saint Mark's, Greenwich Country Day School and Educational Policy Center, among others.

- Having completed the merger of our firm and a painful divorce, I began to think about new opportunities.

- Most important of all – the arrival of three sons who I knew I would love unconditionally always!

- An over-arching responsibility for Matthew and to a very real extent, the broader family as well.

memories of Charleston . . .

- Digesting the fear of a culture shock after deciding to move to Charleston with only three friends in the city (Messrs. Ravenel, Duell, and Manigault).

- Realizing almost immediately that a balance in life between for-profit involvement and not-for-profit involvement gave me a more complete feeling.

- Serving on at least fifteen boards in each category and running a few entities in each created a signal ... not to boast about any achievements – particularly in my adopted city!

- It is axiomatic that achievements or opinions brought to the Holy City are of limited interest (as it is elsewhere!).

- A commitment to the community by outsiders is of interest.

- Gradually finding a level of acceptance only if we behaved ourselves. New doors began to open up in Charleston.

- Moved from 52 King Street to 9 Ladson Street. We built a Widow's Walk on top of our new house.

- Purchased a commercial building at One North Adger's Wharf, intended as an investment for my sons as well as for me. It also provided a place to work following Hurricane Hugo.

- Our new home became a target for gatherings of various not-for-profit events, for parties, for club and society gatherings.

- Monthly visits to see Matthew in Boston became a scheduled project along with business and charity trips to New York.

- A major effort was made to connect with my own family which became more and more challenging as they settled elsewhere.

- With all the good things that developed in Charleston, we missed the cooler weather in the summer and the limited choices in education. We also missed our friends and family.

children . . . a series of

- Dr. Martens introducing me to my eldest son.

- Jay and Gren meet in New York apartment
  for the first time (after Gren's birth).

- Bayard's arrival in Greenwich Hospital delivery
  room (my only son born in New England).

- Teddy's yawn upon his first encounter with me.

- Arizona rides on horseback at our favorite ranch.

- Groton Plantation hunts with BB
  guns, rifles, and shotguns.

- Jay's near drowning incident in our neighbor's pool.

- Gren's near catastrophe with a car running over him.

- Bayard's weight problem ... and
  then a gradual recovery.

- Drugs, motor scooter, cars, and alcohol
  worries of all four sons continuing with
  Teddy (born in June of 1986).

memories

- Jay's entry into the "war zone" of money management, setting up his own firm with Rob Douglass, while Gren and Bayard followed suit by setting up their own companies in Charleston and San Francisco respectively.

- And eventually grandchildren. (Now the circle is complete!)

PART II

Introduction

This book is not a long one; it is not funny, sentimental, or thought-provoking. It is intended to celebrate the years I have shared with my brother. It seems to me that these years are worth a comment or two since we have known each other for a very long time.

Matthew has given me far more than he or anyone may realize. His wonderful sense of humor, often hidden from the outside world, has brought me joy. His endless hours of selecting news items from Boston newspapers have reinforced my ties to the city of our birth – the "Shining City on a Hill," as a famous man once said. His memories of the past have created a strong bond between us.

Finally, Matthew's loyalty and generosity to the few people we have known and trusted have been an inspiration me. I am devoted to Matthew, and he knows that. But it seems appropriate somehow to write this series of letters to him at this late stage of our lives – not only to express devotion, but to paint memory pictures with words.

Dear Matthew,

Now, as you approach your birthday, those of us close to you want to celebrate it and salute you. Perhaps it is worth pausing a moment to describe why you are admired and respected by those of us who have come to know you well.

Despite any problems you may have encountered, you have always concerned yourself with the needs of others – from the days of giving mail and presents to the black people on Groton Plantation as a small boy, to detailing and putting into action a charitable program which is more carefully devised and thoughtfully implemented than most we have known in recent years.

Indeed you have given time and given money and given of yourself again and again and again. We have seen you distracted and upset when a Toastmasters program isn't completed the way it should be; we have seen you anguishing over what kind of present to give another person.

We have known you to spend most of your waking hours thinking about the needs and interests of other people. And through it all, you have never lost your sense of humor nor your sense of loyalty to those who care about you!

Maybe you can better understand why we honor you on your birthday.

Love,

John

Dear Matthew,

Our father, N.T.W. thought that we should go to different schools. This meant that we did not see as much of each other after the divorce. (I will always remember our jokes, mocking self-pity about both of us coming from a broken home!)

In any event, we both went to Dexter School in Brookline, Massachusetts. We went there by bus every morning, dutifully wearing our short visor, crimson Dexter "D" hats.

Among the memories that I retain from those years are the following:

1. You getting the mathematics prize with John Nelson.

2. Bart Harwood (our stepfather) as Chairman of Dexter's Board of Trustees and Francis Caswell, the headmaster of the school, ran our home and the school, respectively, with a very firm hand. Both were feared by both of us.

3. My achievements at Dexter were few. Your performance at Dexter was more to be admired than mine. You were great with numbers and very good at math.

After Dexter you went to Allen Stevenson, Browning, and Solebury School in that order. These were tough years for you and for me. (In fact, we agreed recently that these were the worst years of our lives!) I was struggling at Buckley and Saint Mark's. As "products of a broken home," I am sure that we both suffered from a variety of setbacks. We spent summers in Beverly Farms with our mother and Bart Harwood during these years. Eventually our father began to build a second family.

Love,

John

Dear Matthew,

A long time ago we took a bike ride to New Hampshire together. We had this adventure at a very young age. I couldn't have been more than twelve and you wouldn't have been more than ten years old. I have no idea how those supervising us in Beverly Farms allowed us to do it – to go out on the open roads headed for another state on bicycles. But we did it – peddling northward through the horse country, avoiding major highways, inching our way toward the border. It took us an entire day, but finally we arrived at a bed and breakfast inn at a small town in New Hampshire.

Mercifully, the innkeeper had a room for us and took care of us. The next day we got on our bikes and peddled all the way back home. It seemed a very, very long trip to both of us, but what an adventure it was!

Years later two of my sons, Gren and Bayard, a few years older than we were, had a similar experience – biking across France in the summertime. They found this trip to be a bonding experience just as we did. Perhaps more people should go on bike trips!

Love,

John

Dear Matthew,

It is worth recording a few of the other adventures we shared at an early age ... back in our childhood.

Never will I forget the fun we had throwing snowballs at passing cars in Boston. We stood outside our house and hurled projectiles at unsuspecting drivers on Marlboro Street. The fun stopped when you picked up an ice ball and fired it at a limousine (a "McCann Car," as they were once called). Furious, the driver got out of the car, stormed over to our location and reprimanded us severely.

Years later in another effort to display your pitching prowess with your right arm you broke a window with a tennis ball at our Manchester home, and sometime later you threw green apples at the garage windows of our 143 West Street home in Beverly Farms, Massachusetts. This was shortly before or after the time I shot our neighbor's cat with a twenty-gauge shotgun from the roof of our new home. (I had thought it was not a crime but rather an effort to do our stepfather a favor because he despised cats!) The poor animal, mortally wounded, staggered back to his owner's front porch and expired.

Neither incident improved our relations with our new stepfather – in fact he imposed a set of rules afterwards which you listed sometime ago. Selected rules that you listed will follow in another letter. In a spirit of full disclosure, let it be known that we were very bad boys from time to time during our early years.

Love,

John

Dear Matthew,

Before I forget it I must record for you one of your masterpieces – a partial account of all the rules at the Harwood residence. Some of these were real; some were a bit contrived, but taken in its entirety this creation of yours provided great amusement for all of us. Here goes with a selection of over fifty rules you remembered from the Harwood household:

- Never go on rocks without an adult or John
- No football playing
- No visiting next door neighbors
- No phone calling
- Never hit croquet ball hard
- No matches
- No firecrackers
- No fooling with cigarette lighters
- No toys in closets
- No collecting candy
- No fish in the house which have been caught on the dock
- Make bed every day
- Carry out dishes
- No insects indoors

- No bottle cap collecting
- No spilling of anything
- No bicycle riding (on lawn or estate)
- No apple fights
- Toilets flushed at all times
- No getting on any roofs on Harwood estate
- No running on stairs
- No visiting friend's house overnight

As indicated in an earlier letter, we must have been terribly behaved during our summers in Beverly Farms. While these rules provided great amusement, it must be said that our stepfather and our mother deserved gold stars for putting up with us and adding structure to our dysfunctional lives.

Love,

John

Dear Matthew,

Toastmasters provided a major challenge in your life along with notable achievements. As you know Libby and I were at the event celebrating your loyalty and many years of service to this organization. It was a defining moment for you and for us as well.

Toastmasters created an opportunity to come to grips with the horrors of public speaking. Since I joined the group for a while in Charleston, I also learned the art of avoiding the pitfalls of rambling, fumbling, and feel stupid on my feet. For you it was even more challenging and difficult, I believe.

Nevertheless, you bravely stood before your audience, developed a theme for each delivery, and gave talks again and again and again on a variety of subjects. You made friends; you earned the respect of your fellow Toastmasters; and you developed a sense of self confidence. All your friends were made proud for this big effort of yours and for your many achievements with Toastmasters.

It seems that your work at Toastmasters has received more praise than various other volunteer efforts which include time spent helping less fortunate people at Children's Hospital, Child's Study Association, and Old South Church, among other places – I could write a letter on each of these as well. Let it never be said that Matthew Winthrop never worked! You have paid your dues ... and then some!

Love,

John

Dear Matthew,

You have said, with justification, that many other people do not have any idea about the various drugs you must take to survive each day. For the record, here is the current list:

TEGRETOL – for anti-convulsion

PHENABARBITOL – also to prevent convulsion

LIPITOR – to keep cholesterol under control

CLORAZAPATE – for various neurological disorders

(Dr. Stephen Parker is adjusting all of the above at present.)

Those not taking these drugs have no idea how they can make you dead tired, how they can create various moods, and even how they can make you lose your balance. Perhaps those who don't understand you should pop some of your pills one day. Then they might get the picture. I, for one, am afraid to do it!

Love,

John

Dear Matthew,

The James Bond movies – particularly those featuring Sean Connery – have been high entertainment for both of us. The understated one-liners have always amused us.

Some examples ...

After a long fight with a bad guy, James Bond hurled him into a bathtub full of water. He then threw an electric heater into the water electrocuting the guy on the spot. Dusting off his hands as he walked away, James Bond exclaimed, "Shocking. Absolutely shocking!"

In *Goldfinger* two thugs were tossed into the trunk of a car which, in turn, was brought to a junk heap where the entire car was reduced to a size not bigger than a shoe box by a gigantic crushing machine. When asked where the two gentlemen were, James Bond replied, "They had a pressing engagement!"

In *Thunderball* a man was shot by a blowgun with an arrow. As the victim lay mortally wounded, Bond's comment was, "I think he got the point!" These and many more quips, as well as the joy of seeing "Odd Job" do evil, has kept us smiling for years. Perhaps it is because James Bond movies lift us out of our humdrum lives and give us a very different world from the one we know.

Love,

John

Dear Matthew,

You have survived in apartment 26-F of the Prudential Tower for many, many years. In fact, you must be one of the most loyal and senior residents in that famous building.

Although you never let me visit any more, I can imagine how it must look. Papers piled up in many places, windows sealed shut, relics of the past stored away and the temperature hovering about 90 degrees with you sitting in that blue chair sweating bullets hour after hour.

How you have survived in that claustrophobic environment these many years, I will never know. You remain a unique individual in so many ways.

Stay cool; don't drool; and for God's sake open the window!

Love,

John

Dear Matthew,

We are born alone and we die alone. That's a depressing thought. But the connection with other people during life's journey makes the trip worthwhile.

If I ever feel lonely or alone (and I often do), it must be true with you as well. You have made journeys to Hawaii alone, to Detroit alone, to Iceland alone, to Hong Kong alone, to San Juan and to most of the countries of Europe alone. You even lost your clothes in Southern France and smashed up your car in Detroit! But you have always kept me informed of all aspects of such adventures.

Somewhere, tucked away, I have incredibly long postcards and letters from you describing your trips years ago. In return for your efforts of the past, I would like to put together a description of various voyages I have made over the years. I will present you with a copy if you are interested.

However, the most meaningful and the most recent sharing has been in these past few years when we have spent one evening every month having dinner together and talking over the telephone at the appointed hour at least every week.

All of this, in combination, has been the best of bonding experiences. Indeed, it might be said these are the good old days!

Love,

John

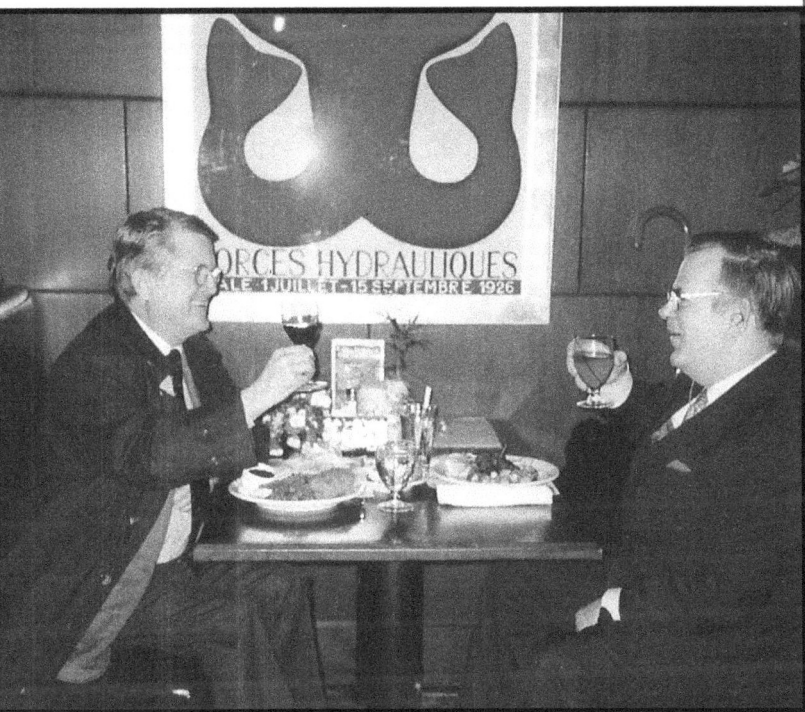

www.ingramcontent.com/pod-product-compliance
Lightning Source LLC
Chambersburg PA
CBHW070830100426
42813CB00003B/559